Table of Contents

Introduction

Propagating plants might sound like a drag, but depending on what type of plant you're working with, it can be simple.

Plant propagation is the process which grows new plants from a variety of sources: seeds, cuttings, and other plant parts. Plant propagation can also refer to the man-made or natural dispersal of seeds.

Propagation is not always successful on the first few tries, but we encourage you start somewhere because it's rewarding when it works! You. Got. This.

Propagation for many plants is best done in potting soil, but some plants can be propagated in water. This is because they have evolved in an environment that allows it. Most Aroid plants can be propagated in water, including pothos plants, philodendrons, monsteras, and ZZ plants. These plants originate from an ancestor that lived in swamps, so being able to adapt to flooding conditions and still being able to grow was key to survival. As a result, the descendants of that ancestor have the ability to grow in water, too. However, they are still land plants and will do best if planted in soil over the long term.

Plant propagation is the process of creating new plants. There are two types of propagation: sexual and asexual. Sexual reproduction is the union of the pollen and egg, drawing from the genes of two parents to create a new, third individual. Sexual propagation involves the floral parts of a plant. Asexual propagation involves taking a part of one parent plant and causing it to regenerate itself into a new plant. The resulting new plant is genetically identical its parent. Asexual propagation involves the vegetative parts of a plant: stems, roots, or leaves.

The advantages of sexual propagation are that it may be cheaper and quicker than other methods; it may be the only way to obtain new varieties and hybrid vigor; in certain species, it is the only viable method for propagation; and it is a way to avoid transmission of certain diseases. Asexual propagation has advantages, too. It may be easier and faster in some species; it may be the only way to perpetuate some cultivars; and it bypasses the juvenile characteristics of certain species.

Sexual Propagation

Seeds and spores can be used for reproduction (through e.g. sowing). Seeds are typically produced from sexual reproduction within a species, because genetic recombination has occurred. A plant grown from seeds may have different characteristics from its parents. Some species produce seeds that require special conditions to germinate, such as cold treatment. The seeds of many Australian plants and plants from southern Africa and the American west require smoke or fire to germinate. Some plant species, including many trees, do not produce seeds until they reach maturity, which may take many years. Seeds can be difficult to acquire and some plants do not produce seed at all. Some plants (like certain plants modified using genetic use restriction technology) may produce seed, but not fertile seed. In certain cases, this is done to prevent the accidental spreading of these plants, for example by birds and other animal.

Sexual propagation involves the union of the pollen (male) with the egg (female) to produce a seed. The seed is made up of three parts: the outer seed coat, which protects the seed; the endosperm, which is a food reserve; and the embryo, which is the young plant itself. When a seed is mature and put in a favorable environment, it will germinate (begin active growth).

Asexual propagation

Plants have a number of mechanisms for asexual or vegetative reproduction. Some of these have been taken advantage of by horticulturists and gardeners to multiply or clone plants rapidly. Humans may utilize these processes as propagation methods, such as tissue culture and grafting. Plants are produced using material from a single parent and as such there is no exchange of genetic material, therefore vegetative propagation methods almost always produce plants that are identical to the parent. Vegetative reproduction uses plants parts such as roots, stems and leaves.

In some plants seeds can be produced without fertilization and the seeds contain only the genetic material of the parent plant. Therefore, propagation via asexual seeds or apomixis is asexual reproduction but not vegetative propagation.

Techniques for vegetative propagation include:

- Air or ground layering
- Division
- Grafting and bud grafting, widely used in fruit tree propagation
- Micropropagation
- Stolons or runners
- Storage organs such as bulbs, corms, tubers and rhizomes
- Striking or cuttings
- Twin-scaling
- Offsets

Heated propagator

A heated propagator is a horticultural device to maintain a warm and damp environment for seeds and cuttings to grow in.

This can be in the form of a clear enclosed bin sitting over a hotpad, or even a portable heater pointed at the bin. The key is to keep the moisture in the clear bin, while keeping lighting over the top of it, usually.

Seed propagation mat

An electric seed-propagation mat is a heated rubber mat covered by a metal cage which is used in gardening. The mats are made so that planters containing seedlings can be placed on top of the metal cage without the risk of starting a fire. In extreme cold, gardeners place a loose plastic cover over the planters/mats which creates a sort of miniature greenhouse. The constant and predictable heat allows people to garden in the winter months when the weather is generally too cold for seedlings to survive naturally. When combined with a lighting system, many plants can be grown indoors using these mats.

What you'll need:

- Plant to propagate
- Scissors
- Glass vessel filled with room temperature water

Step 1

On a mature vine, look right below the leaf or stem/vine juncture for a tiny brown root node. These tiny bumps are the key to propagating pothos. You'll want to snip off a couple inches of healthy stem right before a node and include a node or two with the cutting, as this is where the new roots will come from.

Step 2

Remove any leaves too close to the node, especially ones that might end up submerged under water when you put your cutting into your glass vessel.

Step 3

Place your plant cutting(s) in your glass vessel and put it in a spot that receives bright to moderate indirect light. Do not place in strong, direct light or super-low light.

Step 4

Arguably, the most difficult step: be patient! Check root growth from the node on a weekly basis. Add fresh, tepid water when needed. You can replace the water every few days, or simply top off the vessel with fresh water when it's looking low—as long as there is no murkiness or fungi growing. If the water is murky, we recommend replacing it for the health of the growing root system.

Getting Dirty

If you'd like to transplant your plant cutting(s) from the glass vessel into a planter with potting mix, we recommend waiting until the root is at least 1 inch long or longer. This should take 4-6 weeks. Once the roots of the cutting are potted in fresh potting mix, saturate that mix with room temperature water and place in bright indirect light. Let potting mix dry out between waterings.

Water, Water Everywhere

If you want to keep your plant cutting(s) growing in water indefinitely, that is totally a viable option. A word of warning: the longer your plant cutting sits in water, the worse the plant could fare over time. Why? Water has no nutrients, and can increase the risk for potential fungal infections. You can help to combat this by changing out the water regularly and adding a tiny bit of fertilizer every month or so during the spring and summer growing season.

Seed

To obtain quality plants, start with good quality seed from a reliable dealer. Select varieties to provide the size, color, and habit of growth desired. Choose varieties adapted to your area which will reach maturity before an early frost. Many new vegetable and flower varieties are hybrids, which cost a little more than open pollinated types. However, hybrid plants usually have more vigor, more uniformity, and better production than non-hybrids and sometimes have specific disease resistance or other unique cultural characteristics.

Although some seeds will keep for several years if stored properly, it is advisable to purchase only enough seed for the current year's use. Quality seed will not contain seed of any other crop, weeds, seeds, or other debris. Printing on the seed packet usually indicates essential information about the variety, the year for which the seeds were packaged, and germination percentage you may typically expect, and notes about any chemical seed treatment. If seeds are obtained well in advance of the actual sowing date or are stored surplus seeds, keep them in a cool, dry place. Laminated foil packets help ensure dry storage. Paper packets are best kept in tightly closed containers and maintained around 40∘F. in a low humidity. The door shelves in a refrigerator work well.

Some gardeners save seed from their own gardens; however, such seed is the result of random pollination by insects or other natural agents, and may not produce plants typical of the parents. This is especially true of the many hybrid varieties.

Germination

Germination will begin when certain internal requirements have been met. A seed must have a mature embryo, contain a large enough endosperm to sustain the embryo during germination, and contain sufficient hormones to initiate the process. In general, do not expect more than 65% to 80% of new seeds to germinate. From those germinating, expect about 60% to 75% to produce satisfactory, vigorous, sturdy seedlings. There are four environmental factors which affect germination: water, oxygen, light, and heat.

Water

The first step in the germination process is the imbibition or absorption of water. Even though seeds have great absorbing power due to the nature of the seed coat, the amount of available water in the substrate affects the uptake of water. An adequate, continuous supply of water is important to ensure germination. Once the germination process has begun, a dry period can cause the death of the embryo.

Light

Light is known to stimulate or to inhibit germination of some types of seed. The light reaction involved here is a complex process. Some crops which have a requirement for light to assist seed germination are ageratum, begonia, browallia, impatiens, lettuce, and petunia. Conversely, peas, beans, calendula, centaurea, annual phlox, verbena, and vinca will germinate best in the dark. Other plants are not specific at all. Seed catalogs and seed packets often list germination or cultural tips for individual varieties. When sowing light-requiring seed, do as nature does, and leave them on the soil surface. If they are covered at all, cover them lightly with fine peat moss or fine vermiculite. These two materials, if not applied too heavily, will permit some light to reach the seed and will not limit germination. When starting seed in the home, supplemental light can be provided by fluorescent fixtures suspended 6 to 12 inches above the seeds for 16 hours a day. High intensity lights will provide more light over the course of the day and will enhance the quality of seedlings. These lights cost more than the common shop lights, but are often worth the investment if you plan on growing plants indoors.

Oxygen

In all viable seed, respiration takes place. The respiration in dormant seed is low, but some oxygen is required. The respiration rate increases during germination, therefore, the substrate in which the seeds are placed should be loose and well-aerated. If the oxygen supply during germination is limited or reduced, germination can be severely retarded or inhibited.

Temperature

A favorable temperature is another important requirement of germination. It not only affects the germination percentage but also the rate of germination. Some seeds will germinate over a wide range of temperatures, whereas others require a narrow range. Many seeds have minimum, maximum, and optimum temperatures at which they germinate. For example, tomato seed has a minimum germination temperature of 50 degrees F. and a maximum temperature of 95 degrees, but an optimum germination temperature of about 80 degrees. Where germination temperatures are listed, they are usually the optimum temperatures unless otherwise specified. Generally, 65 to 75 degrees F. is best for most plants. This often means the germination flats may have to be placed in special chambers or on radiators, heating cables, or heating mats to maintain optimum temperature. The importance of maintaining proper substrate temperature to achieve maximum germination percentages cannot be over-emphasized. It's also very important to note that the recommended temperatures need to be maintained 24 hours a day.

Methods of Breaking Dormancy

One of the functions of dormancy is to prevent a seed from germinating before it is surrounded by a favorable environment. In some trees and shrubs, seed dormancy is difficult to break, even when the environment is ideal. Various treatments are performed on the seed to break dormancy and begin germination.

Scarification

Seed scarification involves breaking, scratching, or softening the seed coat so that water can enter and begin the germination process. There are several methods of scarifying seeds. In acid scarification, seeds are put in a glass container and covered with concentrated sulfuric acid. The seeds are gently stirred and allowed to soak from 10 minutes to several hours, depending on the hardness of the seed coat. When the seed coat has become thin, the seeds can be removed, washed, and planted. Another scarification method is mechanical. Seeds are filed with a metal file, rubbed with sandpaper, or cracked with a hammer to weaken the seed coat. Hot water scarification involves putting the seed into hot water (170 to 212 degrees F). The seeds are allowed to soak in the water, as it cools, for 12 to 24 hours and then planted. A fourth method is one of warm, moist scarification. In this case, seeds are stored in nonsterile, warm, damp containers where the seed coat will be broken down by decay over several months.

Stratification

Seeds of some fall-ripening trees and shrubs of the temperate zone will not germinate unless chilled underground as they over winter. This so called "after ripening" may be accomplished artificially by a practice called stratification. The following procedure is usually successful. Put sand or vermiculite in a clay pot to about 1 inch from the top. Place the seeds on top of the medium and cover with ½ inch of sand or vermiculite. Wet the medium thoroughly and allow excess water to drain through the hole in the pot. Place the pot containing the moist medium and seeds in a plastic bag and seal. Place the bag in a refrigerator. Periodically check to see that the medium is moist, but not wet. Additional water will probably not be necessary. After 10 to 12 weeks, remove the bag from the refrigerator. Take the pot out and set it in a warm place in the house. Water often enough to keep the medium moist. Soon the seedlings should emerge. When the young plants are about 3 inches tall, transplant them into pots to grow until time for setting outside.

Another procedure that is usually successful uses sphagnum moss or peat moss. Wet the moss thoroughly, then squeeze out the excess water with your hands. Mix seed with the sphagnum or peat and place in a plastic bag. Seal the bag and put it in a refrigerator. Check periodically. If there is condensation on the inside of the bag, the process will probably be successful. After 10 to 12 weeks, remove the bag from the refrigerator. Plant the seeds in pots to germinate and grow. Handle seeds carefully. Often the small roots and shoots are emerging at the end of the stratification period. Care must be taken not to break these off. Temperatures in the range of 35 to 45 degrees F (2 to 70C) are effective. Most refrigerators operate in this range. Seeds of most fruit and nut trees can be successfully germinated by these procedures. Seeds of peaches should be removed from the hard pit. Care must be taken when cracking the pits. Any injury to the seed itself can be an entry path for disease organisms.

Starting Seeds

Substrate (aka Media)

A wide range of materials can be used to start seeds, from plain vermiculite or mixtures of soilless substrates to the various amended soil mixes. With experience, you will learn to determine what works best for the seeds that you are starting. When choosing a substrate its important to keep in mind what the good qualities of a germinating substrate are. It should be rather fine and uniform, yet well-aerated and loose. It should be free of insects, disease organisms, and weed seeds. It should also be of low fertility or total soluble salts and capable of holding and moving moisture by capillary action. One mixture which supplies these factors is a combination of 1/3 sterilized soil, 1/3 sand or vermiculite or perlite, and 1/3 peat moss.

The importance of using a sterile medium and container cannot be over-emphasized. The home gardener can treat a small quantity of soil mixture in an oven. Place the slightly moist soil in a heat-resistant container in an oven set at about 250 degrees F. Use a candy or meat thermometer to ensure that the mix reaches a temperature of 180 degrees F. for at least 1/2 hour. Avoid over-heating as this can be extremely damaging to the soil. Be aware that the heat will release very unpleasant odors in the process of sterilization. This treatment should prevent damping-off and other plant diseases, as well as eliminate potential plant pests. Growing containers and implements should be washed to remove any debris and rinsed in a solution of 1 part chlorine bleach to 9 parts water.

An artificial, soilless mix also provides the desired qualities of a good germination substrate. The basic ingredients of such a mix are sphagnum peat moss and vermiculite, both of which are generally free of diseases, weed seeds, and insects. The ingredients are also readily available, easy to handle, lightweight, and produce uniform plant growth. "Peat-lite" mixes or similar products are commercially available or can be made at home using this recipe: 4 quarts of shredded sphagnum peat moss, 4 quarts of fine vermiculite, 1 tablespoon of superphosphate, and 2 tablespoons of ground limestone. Mix thoroughly. These mixes have little fertility, so seedlings must be watered with a diluted fertilizer solution soon after they emerge. Do not use garden soil by itself to start seedlings; it is not sterile, is too heavy, and will not drain well.

Containers

Flats and trays can be purchased or you can make your own containers for starting seeds by recycling such things as cottage cheese containers, the bottoms of milk cartons or bleach containers, and pie pans, as long as good drainage is provided. At least one company has developed a form for recycling newspaper into pots, and another has developed a method for the consumer to make and use compressed blocks of soil mix instead of pots. You can make your own flats from scrap lumber. A convenient size to handle would be about 12 to 18 inches long and 12 inches wide with a depth of about 2 inches. Leave cracks of about 1/8-inch between the boards in the bottom or drill a series of holes to ensure good drainage.

Clay or plastic pots can be used and numerous types of pots made of compressed peat and other biodegradable materials are also on the market. Multi-cell containers (packs) where each cell holds a single plant reduce the risk of root injury when transplanting young plants. Peat pellets, peat or fiber-based blocks, and expanded foam cubes can also be used for seeding. The downside to sowing seeds in individual cells or pellets is that they dry out faster than multiple seedlings sown in a flat or larger container.

Seeding

The proper time for sowing seeds for transplants depends upon when plants may safely be moved out-of-doors in your area. This period may range from 4 to 12 weeks prior to transplanting, depending upon the speed of germination, the rate of growth, and the cultural conditions provided. A common mistake is to sow the seeds too early and then attempt to hold the seedlings back under poor light or improper temperature ranges. This usually results in tall, weak, spindly plants which do not perform well in the garden.

After selecting a container, fill it to within ¾ inch of the top with moistened substrate. For very small seeds, at least the top ¼-inch should be a fine, screened mix or a layer of vermiculite. Gently firm the substrate at the corners and edges with your fingers or a block of wood to provide a uniform, flat surface.

For medium and large seeds, make furrows 1 to 2 inches apart and 1/8 to ¼-inch deep across the surface of the container using a narrow board or pot label. By sowing in rows, good light and air movement results, and if damping-off fungus does appear, there is less chance of it spreading.

Seedlings in rows are easier to label and handle at transplanting time than those which have been sown in a broadcast manner. Sow the seeds thinly and uniformly in the rows by gently tapping the packet of seed as it is moved along the row. Lightly cover the seed with dry vermiculite or sifted substrate if they require darkness for germination. A suitable planting depth is usually about twice the diameter of the seed.

Do not plant seeds too deeply. Extremely fine seed such as petunia, begonia, and snapdragon are not covered, but lightly pressed into the medium or watered in with a fine mist. If these seeds are broadcast, strive for a uniform stand by sowing half the seeds in one direction, then sowing the other way with the remaining seed in a crossing pattern.

Large seeds are frequently sown into some sort of a small container or cell pack which eliminates the need for early transplanting. Usually 2 or 3 seeds are sown per unit and later thinned to allow the strongest seedling to grow. A germination test will allow you to determine how many seeds need to be sown per cell. If seeds have a very low germination rate (<40%), sow at least 3 seeds per cell or consider tossing out the seed. For germination rates of 40-80%, sow 2-3 seeds per cell. If you want to be frugal with your seeds, sow only 1 per cell if your rate is over 80%.

Seed Tape

Most garden stores and seed catalogs offer indoor and outdoor seed tapes. Seed tape has precisely spaced seeds enclosed in an organic, water-soluble material. When planted, the tape dissolves and the seeds germinate normally. Seed tapes are especially convenient for tiny, hard-to-handle seeds. However, tapes are much more expensive per seed. Seed tapes allow uniform emergence, eliminate overcrowding, and permit sowing in perfectly straight rows. The tapes can be cut at any point for multiple-row plantings, and thinning is rarely necessary.

Pregermination

Another method of starting seeds is pregermination. This method involves sprouting the seeds before they are planted. This reduces the time to germination, as the temperature and moisture are easy to control. A high percentage of germination is achieved since environmental factors are optimum. Lay seeds between the folds of a cotton cloth or on a layer of vermiculite in a shallow pan. Keep moist, in a warm place. When roots begin to show, place the seeds in containers or plant them directly in the garden. While transplanting seedlings, be careful not to break off tender roots. Continued attention to watering is critical. Some seed companies sell carefully dried pregerminated seeds. They are usually more expensive compared to conventional seeds and their shelf life is relatively short (approximately a month), but it's a convenient way to ensure a relatively high production rate for the seeds being sown.

When planting fresh, pregerminated seeds in a container to transplant in the garden later, place 1 seed in a 2- to 3-inch container. Plant the seeds at only ½ the recommended depth. Gently press a little soil over the sprouted seed and then add about ¼ inch of milled sphagnum or sand to the soil surface. These materials will keep the surface uniformly moist and are easy for the shoot to push through. Keep in a warm place and care for them as for any other newly transplanted seedlings.

A convenient way to plant small, delicate, pre-germinated seeds is to suspend them in a gel. You can make a gel by blending cornstarch with boiling water to a consistency that is thick enough so the seeds will stay suspended. Be sure to cool thoroughly before use. Place the gel with seedlings in a plastic bag with a hole in it.

Squeeze the gel through the hole along a pre-marked garden row. Spacing of seeds is determined by the number of seeds in the gel. If the spacing is too dense, add more gel; if too wide, add more seeds. The gel will keep the germinating seeds moist until they establish themselves in the garden soil.

Watering

After the seed has been sown, moisten the planting mix thoroughly. Use a fine mist or place the containers in a pan or tray which contains about 1 inch of warm water. Avoid splashing or excessive flooding which might displace small seeds. When the planting mix is saturated, set the container aside to drain. The soil should be moist but not wet.

Ideally, seed flats should remain sufficiently moist during the germination period without having to add water. One way to maintain moisture is to slip the whole flat or pot into a clear plastic bag after the initial watering. The plastic should be at least 1 inch from the soil. Keep the container out of direct sunlight; otherwise the temperature may rise to the point where the seeds will be harmed. Many home gardeners cover their flats with panes of glass instead of using a plastic sleeve. Be sure to remove the plastic bag or glass cover as soon as the first seedlings appear. Surface watering can then be practiced if care and good judgment are used.

Lack of uniformity, overwatering, or drying out are problems related to manual watering. Excellent germination and moisture uniformity can be obtained with a low-pressure misting system. Four seconds of mist every 6 minutes or 10 seconds every 15 minutes during the daytime in spring seems to be satisfactory. Bottom heat is an asset with a mist system. Subirrigation or watering from below may work well, keeping the flats moist. However, as the flats or pots must sit in water constantly, the soil may absorb too much water, and the seeds may rot due to lack of oxygen.

Temperature and Light

Several factors for good germination have already been mentioned. The last item, and by no means the least important, is temperature. Since most seeds will germinate best at an optimum temperature that is usually higher than most home night temperatures, special warm areas must often be provided. The use of thermostatically controlled heating cables is an excellent method of providing constant heat.

After germination and seedling establishment, move the flats to a light, airy, cooler location, at a 55 to 60 degree F. night temperature and a 65 to 70 degree F. day reading. This will prevent soft, leggy growth and minimize disease troubles. Some crops, of course, may germinate or grow best at a different constant temperature and must be handled separately from the bulk of the plants.

Seedlings must receive bright light after germination. Place them in a window facing south, if possible. If a large, bright window is not available, place the seedlings under a fluorescent light. Use two 40-watt, cool-white fluorescent tubes or special plant growth lamps. Position the plants 6 inches from the tubes and keep the lights on about 16 hours each day. As the seedlings grow, the lights should be raised.

Transplanting and Handling

If the plants have not been seeded in individual containers, they must be transplanted to give them proper growing space. One of the most common mistakes made is leaving the seedlings in the seed flat too long. The ideal time to transplant young seedlings is when they are small and there is little danger from setback. This is usually about the time the first true leaves appear above or between the cotyledon leaves (the cotyledons or seed leaves are the first leaves the seedling produces). Don't let plants get hard and stunted or tall and leggy.

To transplant, carefully dig up the small plants with a knife or wooden plant label. Let the group of seedlings fall apart and pick out individual plants. Handle small seedlings by their leaves, not their delicate stems. Gently ease them apart in small groups which will make it easier to separate individual plants. Avoid tearing roots in the process. Punch a hole in the medium into which the seedling will be planted (see below for information about media). Make it deep enough so the seedling can be put at the same depth it was growing in the seed flat. Small plants or slow growers should be placed 1 inch apart and rapid-growing, large seedlings about 2 inches apart. After planting, firm the soil and water gently. Keep newly transplanted seedlings in the shade for a few days, or place them under fluorescent lights. Keep them away from direct heat sources. Continue watering and fertilizing as in the seed flats.

Most plants transplant well and can be started indoors, but a few plants are difficult to transplant. These are generally directly seeded outdoors or sown directly into individual containers indoors. Examples include peas, beans, carrots, beets, chard, zinnias and cucurbits, such as melons and squash.

Media for Transplanting

Seedling growing mixes and containers can be purchased or prepared similar to those mentioned for germinating seed. The medium should contain more plant nutrients than a germination mix, however. Some commercial soilless mixes have fertilizer already added. When fertilizing, use a soluble house plant fertilizer, at the dilution recommended by the manufacturer, about every 2 weeks after the seedlings are established. Remember that young seedlings are easily damaged by too much fertilizer, especially if they are under any moisture stress.

Containers for Transplanting

There is a wide variety of containers from which to choose for transplanting seedlings. These containers should be economical, durable, and make good use of space. The type selected will depend on the type of plant to be transplanted and individual growing conditions. Standard pots may be used, but they waste a great deal of space and may not dry out rapidly enough for the seedling to have sufficient oxygen for proper development.

There are many types of containers available commercially. Those made out of pressed peat can be purchased in varying sizes. Individual pots or strips of connected pots fit closely together, are inexpensive, and can be planted directly in the garden. When setting out plants grown in peat pots, be sure to cover the pot completely. If the top edge of the peat pot extends above the soil level, it may act as a wick, and draw water away from the soil in the pot. To avoid this, tear off the top lip of the pot and then plant flush with the soil level.

Community packs are containers in which there is room to plant several plants. These are generally inexpensive. The main disadvantage of a community pack is that the roots of the individual plants must be broken or cut apart when separating them to put out in the garden.

Compressed peat pellets, when soaked in water, expand to form compact, individual pots. They waste no space, don't fall apart as badly as peat pots, and can be set directly out in the garden. If you wish to avoid transplanting seedlings altogether, compressed peat pellets are excellent for direct sowing.

Community packs and cell packs, which are strips of connected individual pots, are also available in plastic and are frequently used by commercial bedding plant growers, as they withstand frequent handling. In addition, many homeowners find a variety of materials from around the house useful for containers. These homemade containers should be deep enough to provide adequate soil and have plenty of drainage holes in the bottom.

Hardening Plants

Hardening is the process of altering the quality of plant growth to withstand the change in environmental conditions which occurs when plants are transferred from a greenhouse or home to the garden. A severe check in growth may occur if plants produced in the home are planted outdoors without a transition period. Hardening is most critical with early crops, when adverse climatic conditions can be expected.

Hardening can be accomplished by gradually lowering temperatures and relative humidity and reducing water. This procedure results in an accumulation of carbohydrates and a thickening of cell walls. A change from a soft, succulent type of growth to a firmer, harder type is desired.

This process should be started at least 2 weeks before planting in the garden. If possible, plants should be moved to a 45 to 50 degree F. temperature indoors or outdoors in a shady location. A cold frame is excellent for this purpose. When put outdoors, plants should be shaded, and then gradually moved into sunlight. Each day, gradually increase the length of exposure. Don't put tender seedlings outdoors on windy days or when temperatures are below 45 degrees F. Reduce the frequency of watering to slow growth, but don't allow plants to wilt. Even cold-hardy plants will be hurt if exposed to freezing temperatures before they are hardened. After proper hardening, however, they can be planted outdoors and light frosts will not damage them.

The hardening process is intended to slow plant growth. If carried to the extreme of actually stopping plant growth, significant damage can be done to certain crops. For example, cauliflower will make thumb size heads and fail to develop further if hardened too severely. Cucumbers and melons will stop growth if hardened.

Propagation of Ferns by Spores

Though ferns are more easily propagated by other methods, some gardeners like the challenge of raising ferns from spores. One tested method for small quantities follows:

Put a solid, sterilized brick (bake at 250 degrees F. for 30 minutes) in a pan and add water to cover the brick. When the brick is wet throughout; squeeze a thin layer of moist soil and peat (1:1) onto the top of the brick. Pack a second layer (about an inch) on top of that. Sprinkle spores on top. Cover with plastic (not touching the spores) and put in a warm place in indirect light. It may take up to a month or more for the spores to germinate. Keep moist at all times. A prothallus (one generation of the fern) will develop first from each spore, forming a light green mat. Mist lightly once a week to maintain high surface moisture; the sperm must be able to swim to the archegonia (female parts). After about three weeks, fertilization should have occurred. Pull the mat apart with tweezers in ¼-inch squares and space them ½-inch apart in a flat containing a 2-inch layer of sand, ¼-inch of charcoal, and about 2 inches of soil/peat mix. Cover with plastic and keep moist. When fern fronds appear and become crowded, transplant to small pots. Gradually reduce the humidity until they can survive in the open. Light exposure may be increased at this time.

Asexual Propagation

Asexual propagation, as mentioned earlier, is the best way to maintain some species, particularly an individual that best represents that species. Clones are groups of plants that are identical to their one parent and that can only be propagated asexually. The Bartlett pear (1770) and the Delicious apple (1870) are two examples of clones that have been asexually propagated for many years.

The major methods of asexual propagation are cuttings, layering, division, budding and grafting. Cuttings involve rooting a severed piece of the parent plant; layering involves rooting a part of the parent and then severing it; and budding and grafting is joining two plant parts from different varieties.

Cuttings

Many types of plants, both woody and herbaceous, are frequently propagated by cuttings. A cutting is a vegetative plant part which is severed from the parent plant in order to regenerate itself, thereby forming a whole new plant.

Take cuttings with a sharp blade to reduce injury to the parent plant. Dip the cutting tool in rubbing alcohol or a mixture of one part bleach : nine parts water to prevent transmitting diseases from infected plant parts to healthy ones. Remove flowers and flower buds from cuttings to allow the cutting to use its energy and stored carbohydrates for root and shoot formation rather than fruit and seed production. To hasten rooting, increase the number of roots, or to obtain uniform rooting (except on soft, fleshy stems), use a rooting hormone, preferably one containing a fungicide. Prevent possible contamination of the entire supply of rooting hormone by putting some in a separate container for dipping cuttings.

Insert cuttings into a rooting medium such as coarse sand, vermiculite, soil, water, or a mixture of peat and perlite. It is important to choose the correct rooting medium to get optimum rooting in the shortest time. In general, the rooting medium should be sterile, low in fertility, drain well enough to provide oxygen, and retain enough moisture to prevent water stress. Moisten the medium before inserting cuttings, and keep it evenly moist while cuttings are rooting and forming new shoots.

Place stem and leaf cuttings in bright, indirect light. Root cuttings can be kept in the dark until new shoots appear.

Stem Cuttings

Numerous plant species are propagated by stem cuttings. Some can be taken at any time of the year, but stem cuttings of many woody plants must be taken in the fall or in the dormant season.

Tip cuttings: Detach a 2 to 6-inch piece of stem, including the terminal bud. Make the cut just below a node. Remove lower leaves that would touch or be below the medium. Dip the stem in rooting hormone if desired. Gently tap the end of the cutting to remove excess hormone. Insert the cutting deeply enough into the media to support itself. At least one node must be below the surface.

Medial cuttings: Make the first cut just above a node, and the second cut just above a node 2 to 6 inches down the stem. Prepare and insert the cutting as you would a tip cutting. Be sure to position right side up. Axial buds are always above leaves.

Cane cuttings: Cut cane-like stems into sections containing one or two eyes, or nodes. Dust ends with fungicide or activated charcoal. Allow to dry several hours. Lay horizontally with about half of the cutting below the media surface, eye facing upward. Cane cuttings are usually potted when roots and new shoots appear but new shoots from dracaena and croton are often cut off and re-rooted in sand.

Single Eye: The eye refers to the node. This is used for plants with alternate leaves when space or stock material are limited. Cut the stem about ½-inch above and ½-inch below a node. Place cutting horizontally or vertically in the medium.

Double Eye: This is used for plants with opposite leaves when space or stock material is limited. Cut the stem about 12-inches above and 12-inches below the same node. Insert the cutting vertically in the medium with the node just touching the surface.

Heel cutting: This method uses stock material with woody stems efficiently. Make a shield-shaped cut about halfway through the wood around a leaf and axial bud. Insert the shield horizontally into the medium.

Leaf Cuttings

Leaf cuttings are used almost exclusively for a few indoor plants. Leaves of most plants will either produce a few roots but no plant, or just decay.

Whole leaf with petiole: Detach the leaf and up to 1 ½ inches of petiole. Insert the lower end of the petiole into the medium. One or more new plants will form at the base of the petiole. The leaf may be severed from the new plants when they have their own roots, and the petiole reused. illustration showing whole leaf cutting with petiole

Whole leaf without petiole: This is used for plants with sessile leaves. Insert the cutting vertically into the medium. A new plant will form from the axillary bud. The leaf may be removed when the new plant has its own roots. illustration showing whole leaf cutting without petiole

Split vein: Detach a leaf from the stock plant. Slit its veins on the lower leaf surface. Lay the cutting, lower side down, on the medium. New plants will form at each cut. If the leaf tends to curl up, hold it in place by covering the margins with the rooting medium. illustration showing split vein cutting

Leaf sections: This method is frequently used with snake plant and fibrous rooted begonias. Cut begonia leaves into wedges with at least one vein. Lay leaves flat on the medium. A new plant will arise at the vein. Cut snake plant leaves into 2-inch sections. Consistently make the lower cut slanted and the upper cut straight so you can tell which is the top. Insert the cutting vertically. Roots will form fairly soon, and eventually a new plant will appear at the base of the cutting. These and other succulent cuttings will rot if kept too moist.

Root Cuttings

Root cuttings are usually taken from 2 to 3 year old plants during their dormant season when they have a large carbohydrate supply. Root cuttings of some species produce new shoots, which then form their own root systems, while root cuttings of other plants develop root systems before producing new shoots.

Plants with large roots: Make a straight top cut. Make a slanted cut 2 to 6 inches below the first cut. Store cutting about 3 weeks in moist sawdust, peat moss, or sand at 40 degrees F. Remove from storage. Insert the cutting vertically with the top approximately level with the surface of the rooting medium. This method is often used outdoors.

Plants with small roots: Take 1 to 2 inch sections of roots. Insert the cuttings horizontally about 12 inches below the medium surface. This method is usually used indoors or in a hotbed.

Layering

Stems still attached to their parent plants may form roots where they touch a rooting medium. Severed from the parent plant, the rooted stem becomes a new plant. This method of vegetative propagation, called layering, promotes a high success rate because it prevents the water stress and carbohydrate shortage that plague cuttings.

Some plants layer themselves naturally, but sometimes plant propagators assist the process. Layering is enhanced by wounding one side of the stem or by bending it very sharply. The rooting medium should always provide aeration and a constant supply of moisture.

The following propagation methods can all be considered types of layering, as the new plants form before they are detached from their parent plants:

Tip layering: Dig a hole 3 to 4 inches deep. Insert the shoot tip and cover it with soil. The tip grows downward first, then bends sharply and grows upward. Roots form at the bend, and the recurved tip becomes a new plant. Remove the tip layer and plant it in the early spring or late fall. Examples: purple and black raspberries, trailing blackberries. illustration showing tip layering

Compound layering: This method works for plants with flexible stems. Bend the stem to the rooting medium as for simple layering, but alternately cover and expose stem sections. Wound the lower side of the stem sections to be covered. Examples: heart-leaf philodendron, pothos. illustration showing compound layering

Mound (stool) layering: Cut the plant back to 1 inch above the ground in the dormant season. Mound soil over the emerging shoots in the spring to enhance their rooting. Examples: gooseberries, apple rootstocks. illustration showing mound layering

Air layering: Air layering is used to propagate some indoor plants with thick stems, or to rejuvenate them when they become leggy. Slit the stem just below a node. Pry the slit open with a toothpick. Surround the wound with wet unmilled sphagnum moss. Wrap plastic or foil around the sphagnum moss and tie in place. When roots pervade the moss, cut the plant off below the root ball. Examples: dumbcane, rubber tree.

Simple layering: Bend the stem to the ground. Cover part of it with soil, leaving the last 6 to 12 inches exposed. Bend the tip into a vertical position and stake in place. The sharp bend will often induce rooting, but wounding the lower side of the branch or loosening the bark by twisting the stem may help. Examples: rhododendron, honeysuckle.

Division

Plants with more than one rooted crown may be divided and the crowns planted separately. If the stems are not joined, gently pull the plants apart. If the crowns are united by horizontal stems, cut the stems and roots with a sharp knife to minimize injury. Divisions of some outdoor plants should be dusted with a fungicide before they are replanted. Examples: dahlias, iris, rhubarb, day lilies.

Separation

Separation is a term applied to a form of propagation by which plants that produce bulbs or corms multiply.

Bulbs: New bulbs form beside the originally planted bulb. Separate these bulb clumps every 3 to 5 years for largest blooms and to increase bulb population. Dig up the clump after the leaves have withered. Gently pull the bulbs apart and replant them immediately so their roots can begin to develop. Small, new bulbs may not flower for 2 or 3 years, but large ones should bloom the first year. Examples: tulip, narcissus.

Corms: A large new corm forms on top of the old corm, and tiny cormels form around the large corm. After the leaves wither, dig up the corms and allow them to dry in indirect light for 2 or 3 weeks. Remove the cormels, and then gently separate the new corm from the old corm. Dust all new corms with a fungicide and store in a cool place until planting time. Examples: crocus, gladiolus.

Grafting

Grafting and budding are methods of asexual plant propagation that join plant parts so they will grow as one plant. These techniques are used to propagate cultivars that will not root well as cuttings or whose own root systems are inadequate. One or more new cultivars can be added to existing fruit and nut trees by grafting or budding.

The portion of the cultivar that is to be propagated is called the scion. It consists of a piece of shoot with dormant buds that will produce the stem and branches. The rootstock, or stock, provides the new plant's root system and sometimes the lower part of the stem. The cambium is a layer of cells located between the wood and bark of a stem from which new bark and wood cells originate.

Four conditions must be met for grafting to be successful: the scion and rootstock must be compatible; each must be at the proper physiological stage; the cambial layers of the scion and stock must meet; and the graft union must be kept moist until the wound has healed.

Cleft grafting: Cleft grafting is often used to change the cultivar or top growth of a shoot or a young tree (usually a seedling). It is especially successful if done in the early spring. Collect scion wood 3/8 to 5/8 inch in diameter. Cut the limb or small tree trunk to be reworked, perpendicular to its length. Make a 2-inch vertical cut through the center of the previous cut. Be careful not to tear the bark. Keep this cut wedged apart. Cut the lower end of each scion piece into a wedge. Prepare two scion pieces 3 to 4 inches long. Insert the scions at the outer edges of the cut in the stock. Tilt the top of the scion slightly outward and the bottom slightly inward to be sure the cambial layers of the scion and stock touch. Remove the wedge propping the slit open and cover all cut surfaces with grafting wax.

Bark grafting: Unlike most grafting methods, bark grafting can be used on large limbs, although these are often infected before the wound can completely heal. Collect scion wood 3/8 to 1/2 inch in diameter when the plant is dormant, and store the wood wrapped in moist paper in a plastic bag in the refrigerator. Saw off the limb or trunk of the rootstock at a right angle to itself. In the spring, when the bark is easy to separate from the wood, make a 12-inch diagonal cut on one side of the scion, and a 1½-inch diagonal cut on the other side. Leave two buds above the longer cut. Cut through the bark of the stock, a little wider than the scion. Remove the top third of the bark from this cut. Insert the scion with the longer cut against the wood. Nail the graft in place with flat-headed wire nails. Cover all wounds with grafting wax.

Whip or tongue grafting: This method is often used for material 1/4 to ½ inch in diameter. The scion and rootstock are usually of the same diameter, but the scion may be narrower than the stock. This strong graft heals quickly and provides excellent cambial contact. Make one 2½-inch long sloping cut at the top of the rootstock and a matching cut on the bottom of the scion. On the cut surface, slice downward into the stock and up into the scion so the pieces will interlock. Fit the pieces together, then tie and wax the union.

Care of the Graft

Very little success in grafting will be obtained unless proper care is maintained for the following year or two. If a binding material such as strong cord or nursery tape is used on the graft, this must be cut shortly after growth starts to prevent girdling. Rubber budding strips have some advantages over other materials. They expand with growth and usually do not need to be cut, as they deteriorate and break after a short time. It is also an excellent idea to inspect the grafts after 2 or 3 weeks to see if the wax has cracked, and if necessary, rewax the exposed areas. After this, the union will probably be strong enough and no more waxing will be necessary.

Limbs of the old variety which are not selected for grafting should be cut back at the time of grafting. The total leaf surface of the old variety should be gradually reduced as the new one increases until at the end of 1 or 2 years, the new variety has completely taken over. Completely removing all the limbs of the old variety at the time of grafting increases the shock to the tree and causes excessive suckering. Also, the scions may grow too fast, making them susceptible to wind damage.

Budding

Budding, or bud grafting, is the union of one bud and a small piece of bark from the scion with a rootstock. It is especially useful when scion material is limited. It is also faster and forms a stronger union than grafting.

Patch budding: Plants with thick bark should be patch budded. This is done while the plants are actively growing, so their bark slips easily. Remove a rectangular piece of bark from the rootstock. Cover this wound with a bud and matching piece of bark from the scion. If the rootstock's bark is thicker than that of the scion, pare it down to meet the thinner bark so that when the union is wrapped the patch will be held firmly in place.

Chip budding: This budding method can be used when the bark is not slipping. Slice downward into the rootstock at a 45 degree angle through 1/4 of the wood. Make a second cut upward from the first cut, about one inch. Remove a bud and attending chip of bark and wood from the scion shaped so that it fits the rootstock wound. Fit the bud chip to the stock and wrap the union.

T-budding: This is the most commonly used budding technique. When the bark is slipping, make a vertical cut (same axis as the root stock) through the bark of the rootstock, avoiding any buds on the stock. Make a horizontal cut at the top of the vertical cut (in a T shape) and loosen the bark by twisting the knife at the intersection. Remove a shield-shaped piece of the scion, including a bud, bark, and a thin section of wood. Push the shield under the loosened stock bark. Wrap the union, leaving the bud exposed.

Care of Buds

Place the bud in the stock in August. Force the bud to develop the following spring by cutting the stock off 3 to 4 inches above the bud. The new shoot may be tied to the resulting stub to prevent damage from the wind. After the shoot has made a strong union with the stock, cut the stub off close to the budded area.